SUPERSTARS OF WRESTLING

THE BIG SHOW

By Ryan Nagelhout

Gareth Stevens
Publishing

RIGHT ON!

Please visit our website, www.garethstevens.com. For a free color catalog of all our high-quality books, call toll free 1-800-542-2595 or fax 1-877-542-2596.

Library of Congress Cataloging-in-Publication Data

Nagelhout, Ryan.
 The big show / Ryan Nagelhout.
     p. cm. — (Superstars of wrestling)
 Includes index.
 ISBN 978-1-4339-8536-2 (pbk.)
 ISBN 978-1-4339-8537-9 (6-pack)
 ISBN 978-1-4339-8535-5 (library binding)
 1. Big Show, 1972—Juvenile literature. 2. Wrestlers—United States—Biography—Juvenile literature. I. Title.
 GV1196.B57N34 2013
 796.812092—dc23
 [B]

                                    2012036994

First Edition

Published in 2013 by Gareth Stevens Publishing
111 East 14th Street, Suite 349
New York, NY 10003

Copyright © 2013 Gareth Stevens Publishing

Designer: Nicholas Domiano
Editor: Ryan Nagelhout

Photo credits: Cover background Denis Mironov/Shutterstock.com; cover, 7, 25 Steve Haag/Getty Images Entertainment/Getty Images; p. 5, 15, 17 Moses Robinson/Getty Images Entertainment/Getty Images; p. 9 Jam Media/LatinContent Editorial/Getty Images; p. 11, 19 Jim R. Bounds/AP Images for WWE; p. 13 J. Shearer/WireImage/Getty Images; p. 21, 23 Ethan Miller/Getty Images Entertainment/Getty Images; p. 27 John Sciulli/Getty Images Sport/Getty Images; p. 29 Johnathan Leibson/FilmMagic/Getty Images.

Printed in the United States of America

CPSIA compliance information: Batch #CW13GS: For further information contact Gareth Stevens, New York, New York at 1-800-542-2595.

Contents

Meet Big Show

Big Show is a giant of the

wrestling world!

Big Show's real name is Paul Donald Wight Jr. He was born on February 8, 1972, in Aiken, South Carolina.

7

Big Boy

Big Show was born with a condition called acromegaly. This made him grow very fast. He had surgery to stop his growth when he was 19.

9

Hoops Show

Big Show is 7 feet tall! He played basketball growing up. He went to Wichita State University to play hoops.

Early Days

Big Show started wrestling in 1994 and soon signed with WCW, a WWE competitor.

Big Show wrestled under the name "The Giant" during his WCW days. He was first billed as the "son" of Andre the Giant.

15

In 1995, he won the WCW title just 6 months after his debut. At age 23, he became the youngest-ever WCW champion.

17

Switching Sides

In 1999, "The Giant" became The Big Show when he joined WWE. He quickly added the WWE Championship to his collection.

19

Big Three

In 2006, Big Show won the ECW Championship. He was the first wrestler to win the WWE, WCW, and ECW titles!

21

Big Show has also won Tag Team titles with wrestlers such as Chris Jericho, The Miz, Kane, and Undertaker.

23

Slime Time

In 2012, Big Show beat The Miz at the Nickelodeon Kids Choice Awards for the Slime Wrestling Championship. He threw The Miz into a pool of slime for the win!

25

Big Role

In 2010, Big Show starred in the movie *Knucklehead*. He has also acted in the movie *Jingle All the Way* and television shows like *Burn Notice* and *Royal Pains*.

27

What's Next?

Big Show is one of the biggest and most successful wrestlers in WWE history. What will he do next?

29

Timeline

1972   Paul Donald Wight Jr. is born on February 8.

1994   Big Show starts wrestling as The Giant.

1995   Big Show is youngest-ever WCW champion.

1999   Big Show signs with WWE and wins title.

2006   Big Show wins ECW title.

2010   Big Show stars in the movie *Knucklehead*.

2012   Big Show wins Slime Wrestling Championship.

For More Information

Books:

Stone, Adam. *The Big Show*. Minneapolis, MN: Bellwether Media, 2012.

Sullivan, Kevin. *Big Show*. New York, NY: DK, 2011.

Websites:

Big Show's Official WWE Page
wwe.com/superstars/bigshow
Find photos, videos, and more of wrestling's grappling giant.

Big Show's Wrestling Profile
onlineworldofwrestling.com/profiles/b/big-show. html
See results from Big Show's matches at his Online World of Wrestling page.

Glossary

acromegaly: a condition that makes someone grow very fast

champion: the overall winner of a contest or event

competitor: something or someone you are playing against

condition: something that limits or restricts

surgery: an operation to help fix something wrong with someone

Index